A HUMANISTIC APPROACH TO CIVILITY AND DIGNITY IN THE WORKPLACE

Published by Jennifer Hancock

Copyright 2021 by Jennifer Hancock

Published 2021

Edition: Kindle

ISBN: 9798369905647

Imprint: Independently published

Title: A Humanistic Approach to Civility and Dignity in the Workplace

Author: Jennifer Hancock

Editor: Desiree Vogelpohl

Publisher: Humanist Learning Systems

This book is also available in print at most online retailers

All rights reserved. No part of this book may be used or reproduced in any manner whatsoever without written permission, except in the case of brief quotations embodied in critical articles or reviews.

In this book we will talk about what civility is and why it's beneficial to you as an individual to behave in a professional, dignified manner with others.

TABLE OF CONTENTS:

TABLE OF CONTENTS: 5

CHAPTER 1: WHY CIVILITY? 7

CHAPTER 2: THE PROBLEM OF ENFORCING CIVILITY 13

CHAPTER 3: FREE SPEECH VS. CIVILITY 17

CHAPTER 4: USING DIGNITY TO CREATE CIVILITY 21

CHAPTER 5: WHAT TO DO WHEN PEOPLE AREN'T CIVIL 27

CHAPTER 6: EXAMPLES OF APPLYING DIGNITY IN THE WORKPLACE: 31

CHAPTER 7: A WORD ABOUT DIGNITY VIOLATIONS 39

CHAPTER 8: EMPATHY AND DIGNITY 45

CHAPTER 9: ABOUT THE AUTHOR 49

~~~~

CHAPTER 1: WHY CIVILITY?

Civility is a formal politeness and courtesy in behavior or speech. Being polite and courteous does have its advantages. My father always said, "if you want to slide through life, try being polite." I agree. I have always found that I accomplish more when I'm nice to people. The problem is that being nice doesn't always work.

How can we be nice and also NOT be a doormat or taken advantage of? What about situations where there are legitimate disagreements? How do we navigate civilly through disagreements if the other person isn't being civil? Should we just give in for the sake of *civility*?

To be honest, I'm not sure that civility is the right term to describe the behavior most companies and professional organizations are looking for. I think there are other terms that are better – like conscientiousness - wanting to do your work well and thoroughly. Or dignified – being able to maintain your composure in difficult circumstances.

What are our goals?

To help us answer the question of *why* civility, I am going to go through a Socratic exercise of asking and answering questions until we get to the core problem that we are looking to solve.

Question: What are the business goals we are trying to accomplish through civility?

The answer is usually because we want to create a positive, inclusive workplace culture.

Why? Because having a positive, inclusive workplace culture leads to better and more effective and ethical problem solving. Solving problems well is what businesses are in the business of doing. If you aren't solving problems well, you won't be in business long.

What are the elements of a positive and inclusive work group?

To create a positive and inclusive work group, we need to:

- Accept people as they are
- Tolerate differences
- Focus on our common ethics
- Intentionally work past disagreements with good will

That's the ideal. The reality is that we humans can be very tribal, and we often treat disagreements not as a valid attempt to create good ethical solutions, but as power plays and evil manipulation, because sometimes that's exactly what is happening.

The problem is when we start thinking in an us vs. them framework when we disagree with a coworker, we move away from good problem solving and we start to justify our own bad behavior. This is why most cultures have some version of The Golden Rule. Do unto others as you would have them do to you.

The admonition is to remember this other person you are disagreeing with is just like you. Instead of arguing, perhaps give them the benefit of the doubt and treat them with dignity and compassion. You may just find when you do this that things get easier and that solutions start to present themselves. This really does work. It's why my dad taught me – to slide through life, try being nice.

When I talk to people who are dealing with difficult disagreements, usually what they want is for me to teach them how to 'fix' the other person or how to outmaneuver the other person. What they don't understand is to do that requires you to behave in a dignified and civil manner. In other words, you have to 'fix' yourself first.

To fix yourself, focus on being conscientious and ethical. Ask yourself: how is my behavior impacting others? The way to create positive workplace cultures is for you to decide to behave in a dignified manner and to treat everyone you deal with with dignity. This requires you to take responsibility for your own behavior.

I promise that when you do this, and you start focusing on being dignified and treating people you are in conflict with with dignity, you will win. If instead of focusing on winning the conflict, you instead focus on creating good solutions to your problems, you will *win*.

Always remember, the conflict over how to solve the problem isn't the problem. The conflict you are experiencing is NOT the problem. The problem you are trying to solve IS the problem. Focus on that and the conflict will go away.

And yes, this is true EVEN when the other person is intentionally trying to sabotage you. I have lived this and done this. It really does work. You can come out of some pretty serious interpersonal conflicts with your dignity and reputation intact, but ONLY if you respond with dignity, conscientiousness, and with a laser-like focus on solving the real problem well and not necessarily your way.

~~~~

CHAPTER 2: THE PROBLEM OF ENFORCING CIVILITY

One of the reasons I want you to think about behaving in a dignified manner is because civility is impossible to enforce. Additionally, enforcing civility is also problematic from a problem-solving standpoint.

It is not unusual for disagreements to be viewed as uncivil when really it is just a disagreement. People may use the concept of civility to tone police a disagreement to shut it down. Meaning if someone is agitated or upset, they may say "I won't listen to you until you are civil." What they are really saying is, I don't want to listen to what you have to say.

This is problematic from a problem-solving standpoint because, honestly, most people don't get upset unless there is a good reason to be upset. Refusing to engage in problem solving with someone who is upset is refusing to solve the problem.

This is why I like the concept of dignity better. That we disagree is fine. That we get upset or emotionally vested in a solution is fine. If I approach whatever the disagreement is with dignity (behaving with dignity myself and treating the other person with dignity), then I can help us work past the disagreement and the perceived problems with "tone" while refocusing the conversation onto collaboratively solving the underlying problem.

To even consider collaborative problem solving, you have to a) let go of your own ego and b) treat the other person as a valued partner.

Let me give you an example.

I was recently collaborating with someone on a written document. I had requested that we use suggestions to collaborate using an online document.

This other person didn't use suggestions, they just completely rewrote the document. They deleted things that I felt were critical to the document. They didn't provide any rationale for their actions. They just deleted things and didn't discuss it or give me an option to advocate for keeping them.

It FELT very disrespectful. Like my opinion didn't matter at all. I felt hurt and like I had been dismissed.

I know this person to be kind-hearted and well-intentioned. I knew they probably had not intended to cause me offense. But I still felt offended. I reminded myself to respond with dignity and to try to treat the other person with dignity.

I wrote to them and explained how their actions were experienced by me. I assured them I understood that was not their intent – but that we needed to come to some agreement on HOW we collaborate so that we both feel included and heard so that we can reach consensus on the writing project.

In other words, I asserted my dignity. I acknowledged their dignity. And then I refocused us both on the problem we needed to solve, which was how to collaborate on this writing project. I did this by inviting them to collaborate with me. I didn't argue. I didn't try to win an argument. I invited this person to collaborate with me as equals.

They responded very well, apologized for how they misunderstood the project, and we quickly came to an agreement on how to move forward. This does work and we were both very happy with the final document. They even thanked me for creating space for them to participate and contribute in such a dignified way.

Most importantly, our relationship is stronger for having gone through this disagreement together. Our trust in one another to treat each other with dignity is what all good collaborative teams are grounded in.

You can't enforce trust. You can't force civility. What you can do is engender trust by treating people with dignity, even people you disagree with and who you feel have hurt you!

~~~~

CHAPTER 3: FREE SPEECH VS. CIVILITY

Another problem with trying to enforce civility, as opposed to dignity, is that it can lead to claims of free speech conflicts. In other words, if you restrict certain types of speech, employees may claim you are restricting their free speech.

Let's make one thing very clear. Freedom of speech is a federal protection. It means the government cannot restrict your speech or put you in jail for unpopular speech. Individuals and companies are not the government. They are under no obligation to tolerate unwanted speech.

Does a workplace or a colleague have to tolerate you saying whatever offensive thing you want to say to them? No, they do not. Your speech may be free, but it is NOT free of consequences.

The government won't put you in jail for saying offensive things, but you can lose your job if you use your speech to break the law by using speech to harass or discriminate against your fellow employees or your customers. Harassment is illegal under both civil and criminal law. There are also workplace protections against discrimination. You getting upset doesn't justify saying mean and untrue things about other people.

Legal arguments aside, if you choose to use your speech to say degrading, dehumanizing things about other people that are not based in fact and that serve no legitimate purpose but to upset other people, you should expect negative consequences from your employer and the other people you work with. In fact, employers have both a moral and legal obligation to stop such speech from occurring in the workplace.

Why this matters

If we are going to create positive and inclusive workplace cultures, any speech that excludes people or dehumanizes them must not be tolerated. Saying something that is racist, sexist, ageist, or whateverist - is NOT a legitimate disagreement.

Legitimate disagreements focus on how best to solve the problem at hand. Racist and otherist comments are designed to exclude people by marking them as *other* as a way to justify excluding them from the problm-solving discussion. Using language to exclude people is harmful to the individuals, to problem solving, and to the organization's ability to operate in a dignified, professional, and collaborative way.

Ironically, intolerant speech should NEVER be tolerated. The way to tell if speech is intolerant is whether the person is making a legitimate point about the problem that needs to be solved – or not.

If not, and they are instead making negative comments about a person they disagree with, they are not engaging in a legitimate disagreement and they are not behaving in a dignified manner. Dignified people focus on solving the problem, NOT on dehumanizing their colleagues.

My point is that people who aren't civil should not be allowed to hide behind free speech rights in a workplace. Don't allow people who aren't being civil to you to demand that you be civil to them or to gaslight people into thinking that their incivility is somehow justified by your incivility to them.

The demand for civility can create a vicious cycle. The way out is to use dignity to create civility. This will allow you to help reset interpersonal problems without falling into a vicious tit for tat cycle of tone policing and incivility.

The next section of this book will go into more detail and will discuss how to use dignity to create civility and how to handle dignity violations in a dignified manner when they occur.

CHAPTER 4: USING DIGNITY TO CREATE CIVILITY

What dignity is and how does it relate to civility? How can we use dignity to deal with civility problems effectively?

In order to have a civil workplace, we need to promote individual dignity. If we help people deal with their own dignity violations we can have a tremendous positive impact. We can hurting others to defend ourselves and can start acting as the dignified and civil individual we all imagine ourselves to be.

What is Dignity?

Many people confuse dignity and respect. They are very, very different.

The material on this chapter comes from the Global Dignity Project: (https://globaldignity.org/)

- Dignity is a feeling in your core
- A belief in your own worth
- A belief in the worth of others

"With dignity, we lead lives of hope, optimism and compassion, guided by a universal ethical compass. Dignity is the belief that our basic humanity is shared with every other person on this planet." They go on to say: "We are all born with dignity. It cannot be taken away from us. It is core to our identity and our self-worth." - Global Dignity Project

Respect, on the other hand, is earned. "Respect is something you are given by others because they like what you are doing or how you are behaving or because of something you accomplished."

And yes, most of us want to be respected by our peers. The point is that you can treat people you don't respect with dignity. People who are respected aren't necessarily acting with dignity.

"Like any skill, dignity must be practiced. Cultivating our own dignity awareness helps us stay true to our core when someone does us harm. Think about why people like Gandhi, Rosa Parks, Nelson Mandela, and Malala Yousafzai are so respected: their fights for human rights are rooted in compassion and love, not revenge and hate." - Global Dignity Project

Elements of Dignity

What does it mean to act with dignity? What are the elements of dignity?

Donna Hicks, the author of Leading with Dignity, lists 10 essential elements of dignity. (https://drdonnahicks.com/books/leading-with-dignity/)

Dr. Hicks explains that when we honor someone's dignity, we:

1. Accept their identity and give them the freedom to express their authentic selves without fear of being negatively judged.
2. Recognize their unique qualities, talents, and ways of life, and give them credit for their contributions, ideas, and experience.
3. Acknowledge them and make them feel seen and heard. We validate and respond to their concerns and what they have been through.
4. Include them and make them feel that they belong and are part of a community.
5. Make them feel safe — both physically and from fear of being shamed or humiliated.
6. Treat them fairly and with equality.

7. Give them a sense of freedom and independence and empower them to experience a sense of hope and possibility.
8. Seek understanding and give them the chance to explain their experiences and perspectives.
9. Give them the benefit of the doubt by starting with the premise that they have good motives and are acting with integrity.
10. Apologize and take responsibility when we have violated their dignity. We make a commitment to change hurtful behaviors.

Notice that all these 10 elements are focused on how YOU behave and how YOU respond. Part of being dignified is accepting others and that means accepting that others may not be behaving in an ideal way.

I will talk more about how to respond in a dignified way when other people are not behaving civilly or dignified. Hint, it involves you staying true to your values and maintaining YOUR dignity.

Being dignified is about personal responsibility. It's how you choose to respond to difficult situations. In order to be dignified, you have to give dignity to others. That means treating people you don't currently respect with dignity. It means responding to difficult people with dignity and giving them the benefit of the doubt. I will explain exactly how this helps you in the next chapters.

This doesn't mean you allow unscrupulous people to run roughshod over you. It means you respond with dignity and ethically. If you fail to respond with dignity and fail to treat other people with dignity, you will NOT be dignified.

Finally, understand that you are in control of your own dignity. No one can take your dignity away from you. They may treat you with disrespect, but how you choose to respond is up to you.

~~~~

CHAPTER 5: WHAT TO DO WHEN PEOPLE AREN'T CIVIL

Behaving in a dignified way to people who aren't being civil gives you several advantages. This is about how you choose to respond. Not getting drawn into an unnecessary conflict is benefit number one.

Don't turn what is happening into a conflict. Uncivil people love conflicts. It helps them justify their uncivil behavior. Don't give them that.

If you remain dignified and refuse to fight, but instead keep refocusing on effective, ethical problem solving, you take away their main weapon for getting what they want: an argument and belligerence. The only way to win against such people is to not fight them. Let them fight themselves.

The second benefit is knowing you aren't part of the problem. Behaving with dignity means embodying your values even in difficult situations. Giving dignity to others, behaving ethically, and focusing on problem solving – not conflict – helps you feel good about yourself even when you are being attacked.

I can't overstate this. This is something you do for you because it helps you respect yourself. And that in turn helps you feel dignified and that helps you behave in a dignified way. Think of this as a self-reinforcing virtuous cycle.

The third benefit is that by giving dignity, you diffuse situations and help refocus on effective, collaborative problem solving. This in turn helps solve the problem. Anytime you can help solve a problem ethically and effectively – you will a) have solved the problem and b) behaved in a way that IS worthy of respect.

Let me give you a concrete example of what it looks like when you use dignity to your advantage.

One-sided Fighting

One-sided fighting is bullying. Bullying is bad. Everyone knows it is bad. When someone is being aggressive and NOT engaging in collaborative problem solving, they may be trying to bully their way to their preferred solution.

If you don't fight them, but instead calmly and compassionately keep trying to redirect to collaborative problem solving, it becomes obvious to everyone that the other person - who keeps ranting and raving - IS the problem.

If you rant and rave back at them, you keep everyone else, including yourself, from seeing that. Worse, you create justification in the other person's mind that their ranting and raving at you is totally justified. The people watching your performance will blame you both for not being professional and dignified.

If instead, one of the two people remains calm, civil, dignified, and doesn't hit back but simply says "I understand, let's try to fix this," and keeps trying to redirect the conversation to a productive, collaborative conversation, then it's clear to EVERYONE who the problem is. This other person either stops fighting and starts collaborating or they lose the respect of their peers.

My mother always said, "it takes two people to fight." Don't fight. Don't be part of that problem. If the other person wants to act that way, that is on them. You remain dignified and professional, and you will reap the rewards of being seen as dignified and professional.

~~~~

CHAPTER 6: EXAMPLES OF APPLYING DIGNITY IN THE WORKPLACE:

To help you understand how dignity can help you deal with difficult people and incivility in the workplace, here are three examples from my own life and how I dealt with these individuals using dignity and compassion as my guide.

The Volunteer From Hell

In my first job out of college, I was hired to be the director of volunteer services for the Los Angeles SPCA. I inherited 10 volunteers who thought their job was to spy on staff. I immediately gave them new job descriptions and trained them on the work we wanted them to do. I then paired them with staff members willing to work on repairing the strained staff volunteer relationships and off we went. All but one of the volunteers loved the new work and their staff partners, and things were great.

Except for the one who didn't like what was going on at all. She refused to be part of the new volunteer system – so I fired her. Yes, you can fire volunteers. What happened next was six months of hell. She recruited other directors (my colleagues) and she spread rumors about me. I was accused of sexual misconduct. My looks and clothing were gossiped about and apparently viewed by some as unprofessional. She did everything she could to try and ruin my reputation and get me fired. I'm not going to lie; it was pretty horrible to go through that sort of sustained personal attack on your character.

How did I survive this? By acting as if this person's opinion didn't matter. Because it didn't. I focused on doing my job well. Making sure the people I was working with were being treated with dignity and that our volunteers and staff were working well together. That's it. That's all I did. I didn't respond to any of the allegations, I just did my job professionally, ethically, and effectively.

Eventually my boss was forced to deal with all of this. I asked him to have the people complaining about me put their complaints in writing and attach their names to it, which they did. And then we addressed and put to bed every single rumor about me that had been made. All of them were false and lies and easily proven at that. And that was the end of it.

At no point did I need to "fight" this woman. I just was a good person doing a good job with dignity. And it was so clear that was the case that the rumors just fell away once they were brought into the light. My relationships with the other directors immediately improved and the volunteer program grew until every part of our agency was working with volunteers.

I won by not fighting. I won by remaining dignified in all that I did, and most importantly, by fixing the problems ethically and effectively.

Working with Passive-Aggressive People

One time I worked with a passive-aggressive person. It was very frustrating. Everyone knew she was passive aggressive because everyone had problems working with her because her office was like a black hole of information. She would ask for help on something and then not provide you with the resources you needed to do the work she had just asked you to do. Then she would try to blame you for not getting the work done.

How did I handle this with dignity? Well, it's a long story that ends with her being fired. I never called her out or argued with her about anything. I just put everything we discussed in writing. If she asked for help on something, I would agree to help and lay out what I needed to get the work done in writing, which she would have to agree to *in writing*. And when it didn't materialize, it was obvious where the holdup was.

That's all I did. I didn't let her hide. I didn't argue. I didn't fight. I didn't make it personal. I just did my job professionally, ethically, and with dignity. She was not professional or ethical and that became clear to everyone.

My only sin, if you can call it that, was not saving her from herself. I didn't cover for her. I didn't argue that she was horrible. I simply approached every interaction with her in dignified problem-solving mode.

I treated her with dignity even though she wasn't treating anyone else with dignity. I gave her every opportunity to change her dynamic and she refused and fought everything. That is on her, not on me. Had she taken my hand and worked with me collaboratively, ethically, and professionally – she would not have sunk her career.

As it was, she ended up getting fired by our board of directors who called me prior to firing her to let me know that I had their full support. I did not ask them to fire her. I wasn't involved in any political maneuverings. They could see what was going on by virtue of me not fighting with her, but simply trying to do my job in the most ethical and dignified way. Because I was treating her with dignity, it became clear to everyone else that she was the problem.

Caution - You Won't Always Win

I just gave you two examples where behaving in a dignified and ethical way worked. Now let me give you an example where it didn't, because the reality is doing the right thing sometimes isn't enough.

In one of my jobs, my boss was a racist and sexist pig. I don't use those terms lightly. This is a man who would lean back in his chair and rub his genitals in front of me whenever I would try to talk to him about work-related matters in his office. It was disgusting.

That didn't deter me from doing my job. What caused me to get angry was when he said something incredibly and unapologetically racist in front of me. It was so bad that our customers – from the Philippines – had no idea what he was talking about, but they could tell it was racist, so they looked at me for panicked clarification. I translated what my boss had tried to say into nonracist language, and they were relieved. After our guests left, I confronted my boss and told him as calmly as I could (which wasn't very calm) to never say anything racist in front of me ever again. I then went to his boss and told him what had happened.

Two weeks later my position was eliminated. They could not fire me because I had not done anything wrong. All they could do was eliminate my position. I don't regret anything. I didn't "win" but that's ok. I stood up for what was right with dignity.

In hindsight, I should have reported his obnoxious sexual behavior towards me earlier, but honestly it was so odd, and it didn't negatively impact me so I didn't do anything about it. But if I had, it probably would not have made a difference in that company anyway. Sometimes, the "big boss" just prefers unethical, undignified people. If that is the case, you are better off finding work elsewhere, which is what I did.

Don't Be Scared and Don't Assume the Worst

I just relayed to you three really harrowing situations where people didn't just behave poorly, they were really, truly horrible. Understand that these are extreme cases. I am now in my mid 50's and in my entire career, I've known maybe five people who didn't behave civilly or ethically. The rest – all did. Most people really are well intentioned.

When you have a conflict with someone, remind yourself to step back emotionally and recommit to behaving with dignity and treat the other person with dignity. When I do this, I usually find out that the assumptions I was making about the other person were wrong. Giving dignity means being willing to find out you were wrong and giving the other person the benefit of the doubt so that you can reset the dynamic. This usually works really well.

In the few cases where it doesn't, behaving with dignity will help you get through that with your dignity intact and the self-respect that comes from knowing that you behaved ethically despite being in a truly difficult situation.

~~~~

CHAPTER 7: A WORD ABOUT DIGNITY VIOLATIONS

What are dignity violations and how do we respond to them?

Donna Hicks, whose book I mentioned earlier on the Elements of Dignity, is a peace negotiator. She has worked with Bishop Desmund Tutu on peace accords between different groups. Groups that have literally been killing each other.

Her insight into what she calls Dignity Violations is really interesting and important. She says the first thing that has to happen is to acknowledge each other's dignity. This is hard to do because we are so busy defending our own dignity that we tend to ignore the dignity of others. Specifically, we have to deal with our own dignity violations before we can engage with others and deal with theirs.

Until this happens, people are just talking past each other. Each side citing the various and multiple ways their dignity has been violated and refusing to acknowledge anything else until and unless their dignity violations are recognized, apologized for, and fixed.

This happens over and over and over again. Once you understand what a dignity violation is and how important it is in conversations, disagreements, and conflicts – it will change how you approach everything.

We all feel violated when we feel our dignity as a human being has been violated. For example, if someone bullies us, humiliates us, or treats us as an object and not as a person. If we are degraded or dehumanized, we are treated as less than fully human – that violates our sense of dignity. And it hurts.

It is easy to see how, in a conflict, people feel their dignity has been violated. Because it has been. When we are in conflict with someone, we are rarely treating them as human. We often treat them as a caricature. We might treat them as a demon. We do this because it helps us rationalize our anger and frustration. The danger is that it is easier to be mad at people, angry at them, and to justify harming them in retaliation when we cease to view them as fully human.

This is what distinguishes a conflict from a disagreement. A disagreement is a discussion between people. A conflict is a moral battle between good and evil, with you being good and the other person being evil. Evil beings aren't human, and they deserve whatever bad things happen to them.

And yes, I know you've had these thoughts. We all have. That's the point. To get past this and back into a position of dignity for ourselves, we need to acknowledge our own hurt and the ways we feel our dignity has been violated.

Your dignity has ABSOLUTELY been violated at some point. Possibly recently. Acknowledge that to yourself. Then remember the other person can't take away your dignity. YOU control your dignity. Yes, it hurts, but you are still fully human and still have dignity – if YOU choose to respond with dignity.

The next step is to then acknowledge that the other person is ALSO experiencing dignity violations. If you feel tempted to compare and contrast dignity violations and to assert that yours are worse than theirs, stop and reset. This is NOT a competition you need to win.

Even if your dignity has been violated worse than the other person's, it doesn't matter. What matters is that both you and the other person think your personal dignity violations are the only thing that really matters.

When you acknowledge both your violations and the other person's violations, you accept that both parties are hurt. You understand that both parties need healing. This is where things start to change. You can both protect yourself and help the other person heal. Maybe not right away, maybe not ever. This process takes time. No peace accord happens just because you sit people in a room together. The process takes time because it takes time to develop trust.

By acknowledging the dignity violations, you experienced and letting go of your hurt, it allows you to get to a state where you CAN acknowledge the other person's hurt and can apologize for your role in hurting them. To do this, it's important to realize that they didn't take away your dignity. You still have your dignity.

When you acknowledge your role, it doesn't mean that your dignity violation doesn't matter. It's just an acknowledgement of the hurt the other person is experiencing. That acknowledgement helps build trust.

It's usually at this point those conflicts turn back into collaborative discussions and people can move past the hurt and start focusing on mutually acceptable solutions to the problem. If you insist on holding onto and nursing your wounds, you won't ever get there.

Being the Bigger Person

Being the bigger person means understanding that you are in control of your dignity and that you have the capacity to be compassionate with other people while holding your ground on what you need. Doing so in a way that does not harm the other person, but instead brings them into your circle of compassion and helps them see you as part of their circle of compassion changes everything. It helps them want to work with you on a solution which ends the hurt for both of you. I realize that sounds pie in the sky – but it really does work.

The final thing I want to leave you with is this. When you encounter someone who is behaving badly, understand that they are behaving that way because they are hurting. They are hurting others in a misguided attempt to protect themselves. Don't take what they are doing personally. Their behavior is about them. Don't tolerate bad behavior, but don't take it personally either.

This mindset really will help you focus on problem solving in a compassionate way and help you avoid unnecessary fights. It really will.

CHAPTER 8: EMPATHY AND DIGNITY

I want to leave you with a quote from Brené Brown, a professor of social work at the University of Houston. She said, "In order to empathize with someone's experience you must be willing to believe them as they see it and not how you imagine their experience to be."

A big part of my practice as a Humanist is to accept other people as fully human. That means they are autonomous. They aren't me. They don't think like me. They don't have my experiences and I don't have their experiences. However, they came to be who they are in this minute, I can't possibly imagine. They've had their own journey to get to this point. So, have I.

This knowledge helps me be present for them and hold space for them as the unique and amazing individual they are. Even if I disagree with them. Even if I don't currently "respect" them. I don't need them to be anyone other than who they authentically are. I am confident in my history and experiences that have led me to this point, that their being different doesn't threaten me.

Being willing to learn about and be present for them is a gift I give myself. It helps me to feel connected in the moment and that helps me be more authentic. By honoring their dignity, I honor my own. This honoring the dignity of the other person usually helps the other person see me as a potential ally and supporter so that we can communicate.

By me giving them what they need, dignity, they are now able to reciprocate it to me. If they don't, that's okay too. I don't need to "win." I don't enter these experiences with a win or lose mindset.

By me focusing on their dignity, the entire interaction is transformed. My goal is to understand this person as they understand themselves. This is about learning from the other person. And even if common ground is not achieved, I can use that information in the future to help create strategies that address the very real concerns and needs of people other than myself.

I can't control what other people do. I can only control myself. The act of treating people with dignity is what gives my life dignity and purpose. And that's enough.

Dignity and Civility is not just good personal practice, it's good for business.

There is a great ted talk on the importance of civility and how it's good for business.

Civility and dignity - isn't just about being nice to each other, though ... that is nice. It's also about how we deal with and cope with people who are different than us.

Diversity is important and it's good for business. Not in a "woke" way, but because diverse communities are thriving communities.

It's pretty clear that in places in the US where diversity is the norm, you have booming economies. The economically depressed areas of the countries - are way more homogenous. This pattern holds everywhere in the country.

Diversity is difficult. Dealing with people who don't share our backgrounds, religions or ethnicity, is difficult. And yet, most of us navigate that just fine - by being civil to each other. Through civility - we recognize our common humanity and dignity and the worth of the people we are interacting with.

That civility - allows us to work together and through that work - exchange goods and services with people who are different from us. It allows us create and generate wealth - separately - yet together. Why? Because we aren't artificially restricting our customer base!!!!

It all comes down to social trust. Civility and dignity help create trust. In places where basic levels of dignity and civility are absent, are economically stifled and rife with abuse. The result - depressed economic activity as the building blocks for economic activity, trust, are absent.

Diversity isn't just a moral good. It's an economic good. To get there - we need to not just be more civil - we must recognize the dignity of everyone we work with and all our customers. This is why humanistic management and humanistic businesses and a humanistic economy is so important.

~~~~~

CHAPTER 9: ABOUT THE AUTHOR

Jennifer Hancock is the author of several best-selling and award-winning books and is the founder of *Humanist Learning Systems*. Not only was she raised as a Humanist, she is considered one of the top speakers and writers in the world of Humanism today. Her professional background is varied including leadership positions in both the for-profit and non-profit sectors.

She teaches Humanism – a combination of Love, Rationality, Science, and Responsibility. Her courses will give you hope. It will help you simplify your life by reducing complexity of the problems you face, which will in turn – help you reduce your anxiety. Finally, because this is all science based, it will work.

What makes her unique is that she teaches humanistic approaches grounded in dignity and compassion, coupled with science-based behavioral modification techniques to create positive workplace cultures that eliminate unwanted behaviors like bullying, harassment, and discrimination, while positively reinforcing the behaviors you do want.

Ms. Hancock has a BA in Liberal Studies from the University of Hawaii at Manoa (1990). Her field of study combined cognitive linguistics, anthropology, and psychology. While in college, she apprenticed as a dolphin trainer for a dolphin language/cognition laboratory which is where she learned the behavioral science and behavior modification techniques she now teaches.

Ms. Hancock has worked in executive leadership roles her entire career (since graduating college in 1990). She has literally never not worked in leadership/management. In the course of her career, she has provided training to companies all over the world for both executive leadership as well as staff. She started training and coaching staff in her first job out of college as the director of volunteer services for the Los Angeles SPCA, and has provided training, support, and mentoring programs at every job she's held since, including her stint as the manager of acquisition group information for a 1/2 billion dollar company.

She has over 30 years of experience working in executive leadership and in providing leadership and management training to others. If you let her, she can teach you how to be a more authentic and effective leader who is both powerfully ethical and armed with the technical skills required to master whatever challenges you face with grace and dignity.

Check out her courses and books below to see how she can help you.

More Learning from Jennifer Hancock

OTHER BOOKS BY JENNIFER HANCOCK

- Applied Humanism: How to Create More Ethical and Effective Businesses

- Humanistic Conflict Management

- The Humanist Approach to Happiness

- Jen Hancock's Handy Humanism Handbook

- The Bully Vaccine

- The Humanist Approach to Grief and Grieving

- How to Win Arguments Without Arguing

- Ending Harassment & Retaliation in the Workplace

- Why Bullies Bully & How to Stop Them Using Science

- Reality-Based Decision Making for Effective Strategy Development

- How to De-escalate Conflicts Using Behavioral Science

- Why Conflict Management Doesn't Work

- How to Prevent Passive Aggressive People from Wreaking Havoc in the Workplace
- How to Handle Cranky Customers
- How to Humanistically Handle Bad Bullying Bosses
- Why is Change so Hard?
- Planning for Personal Success

COURSES TAUGHT BY JENNIFER HANCOCK

- Workplace Bullying for HR professionals
- Living Made Simpler
- An Introduction to Humanism
- Socratic Jujitsu: How to Win Arguments Without Argument
- Why Conflict Resolution Doesn't Work When the Problem is Bullying
- Bridging the Generational Divide: Millennials vs. Boomers
- Ending Harassment and Retaliation in the Workplace

- Reality-Based Decision Making for Effective Strategy Development
- How to De-escalate Conflicts Using Behavioral Science
- Why is Change so Hard?
- Principles of Humanistic Management
- 7 Sins of Staff Management
- How to Handle Cranky Customer Problems
- New Manager Orientation
- Humanist Group Leadership Lessons
- Sexual Harassment Training That Works – General
- Sexual Harassment Training That Works – AB 1825
- Stop Bullying in our Workplace – Staff Training
- Sexual Harassment Compliance Training
- No Fear Act Training
- Planning for Personal Success!
- Talking to Your Child About Death
- The Bully Vaccine Toolkit
- How to Talk to Your Child's School About Bullying

- Why Bullies Bully & How to Stop Them
- Humanistic Conflict Management
- Applied Humanistic Leadership

The End

#####

www.ingramcontent.com/pod-product-compliance
Lightning Source LLC
Chambersburg PA
CBHW050312220526
45465CB00005B/1955